Lena Linden

The basic theories of language acquisition

Lena Linden

# The basic theories of language acquisition

GRIN Verlag

Bibliografische Information der Deutschen Nationalbibliothek: Die Deutsche Bibliothek
verzeichnet diese Publikation in der Deutschen Nationalbibliografie; detaillierte bibliografische Daten sind im Internet über http://dnb.d-nb.de/ abrufbar.


1. Auflage 2007
Copyright © 2007 GRIN Verlag
http://www.grin.com/
Druck und Bindung: Books on Demand GmbH, Norderstedt Germany
ISBN 978-3-638-91156-6

# The Basic Theories of
# Language Acquisition

Paper for the seminar 'First Language Acquisition'
University of Cologne
WS 2007

by
Lena Linden

7. Fachsemester
07.03.2007

# Table of Contents

# I.    Introduction

The question how a child's first language is acquired puzzles parents as well as linguists and psychologists, especially because children seem to solve this complex task so fast and seemingly effortless. There are many co-existing views and opinions concerning the issue of language acquisition, some complementary and some mutually excluding each other. Central in the debate on how the native language is acquired is the question of 'nature or nurture'. Is there some inborn human capacity, which enables or facilitates language acquisition or is it just based on the influences of the environment?

The general 'nature or nurture' debate, concerned with the question whether humans are mainly influenced by their genetic predispositions or a product of their environment, has been going on for a long time, already. While, for example, Francis Galton (1870), a cousin of Charles Darwin, favoured the 'nature' point of view, the Behaviourist John Watson (1930) thought humans were only influenced by their environment. He believed that all differences between human beings were caused solely by personal experiences and what they learned from them. He even stated that if he was given a dozen healthy babies, no matter of which origin, he could make each of them become as he intended, just by varying their environment. (Lefrancois, p. 21f) In the context of linguistics, especially research in language acquisition, this question is of particular interest, as some phenomena seem hard to explain without assuming some kind genetic endowment for language acquisition, but, on the other hand, it is not easy to find convincing evidence for this assumption.

Most of the concepts and theories explaining how native languages are acquired go back to three different approaches put forward by Burrhus Federic Skinner, Noam Chomsky and Jean Piaget, either by using their ideas as a starting point or by rejecting them and formulating a new or altered Hypothesis.

This paper will try to present those three basic theories, also taking into account the contexts out of which they emerged, as to fully understand linguistic, like any other scientific, views and theories, they have always to be evaluated with respect to the scientific and cultural background they appeared in.

First it will try to show how Skinners concept of 'verbal behavior' with respect to language acquisition emerged in the development of behaviouristic theories. This will be followed by Chomsky's criticism of Skinner's ideas, leading to his own theory of language and language acquisition, which will be presented. Jean Piaget offers a cognitive approach to the question. His view will be described before comparing nativist and cognitivist ideas, concerning the points whether or not innate structures exist and in how far linguistic and cognitive development are interrelated, taking the opposed views of Piaget and Chomsky, the forerunners of many other important linguists, as an example.

## II.    B.F. Skinners behaviouristic approach

### a    Behaviorism

The term "Behaviorism" was coined by John B. Watson (1913), who based his research on Ivan Pawlow's findings concerning classical conditioning. Behaviourism is concerned with the objective and observable components of human behaviour and how it can be caused or changed. The overall aim of Behaviourism is to discover laws, which rule the relationship between stimuli and specific responses (reactions), taking into account resulting consequences. (Lefrancois, p.15, 17) According to behaviourist theories, learning is a change of behaviour induced by experience. (Lefrancois, p.30)

The most famous example of Classical Conditioning is 'Ivan Pawlow's dog'. Pawlow found out that some dogs in his laboratory did not only secrete saliva when they were fed, but that they started to do so even a bit earlier. In his following experiments, Watson showed that not only seeing the food caused secretion but also certain other stimuli, like a ringing bell, can have the same effect, if the incidents co-occurred often enough.

In these experiments, the food is the 'unconditioned stimulus' and the original 'response' was secretion. This reaction is natural, 'unconditioned', and therefore has not to be learned. If a bell is rang while feeding, as a 'conditioned stimulus', this bell alone can cause the dog to secrete saliva after a certain time, this being now a 'conditioned response'. This way of learning is called 'learning by stimulus substitution'. (Lefrancois, p.17f)

John Watson found out that classical conditioning does not only work with animals, but also with humans. He made 'Little Albert', an orphan boy who had to stay in hospital, fear his white pet rat, by using a frightening noise as unconditioned stimulus and he showed that also the need to urinate and the width of human vessels can be conditioned. (Lefrancois, p. 20f)

Further important contributions to this field of research were made by Edward Thorndike. He said that an organism, faced with a given situation, will respond in several ways, based on a trial and error strategy. If the first reaction leads to a positive, satisfying result, a neurological connection will emerge, which increases the probability of reacting to this stimulus in the same way,

again. If the first reaction does not lead to a satisfying result the organism will go on trying other possible reactions. The more often a certain response follows a given situation, the deeper 'engraved' is the neurological connection, the organism 'learns'. When this connection is not used repeatedly or negative consequences follow the learned behaviour, the connection will fade away, the organism will 'forget'. It is also possible to transfer habitual reactions to new but similar situations, generalizing behaviour. (Lefrancois, p. 26ff) His theory of stimulus-response relations as neurological connections is called 'Connectionism'. In contrast to Pawlow and Watson, Thorndike emphasized the importance of the consequences that follow a reaction. Reactions which co-occur with a satisfying situation increase the probability of the reaction to be repeated while a negative situation will diminish it. This idea of reward and punishment was highly important for the development of further learning theories. (Lefrancois, p. 26)

## b    Skinner's Theory

Burrhus Skinner's 'Operant Conditioning' is based on the theory of Classical Conditioning. He was of the opinion, that only a small percentage of human and animal behaviour could be explained with this approach, as many occurring reactions would not follow clearly defined stimuli. This is why stimuli are not of much relevance in his learning theory. (Lefrancois, p. 32f) Skinner distinguishes two kinds of reactions: respondents and operants. Respondents are reactions to a stimulus, the organism directly responds to its environment. He calls this classical Stimulus-Response Conditioning 'Type S Conditioning'. In addition to these respondents there are operants, reactions occurring without a stimulus. The organism deals with its environment in an active way. When these spontaneous reactions to a situation occur they can be altered through 'reinforcement'. Skinner labels this kind of conditioning 'Type R Conditioning'. (Lefrancois, p. 33)

If the reaction to some situation is followed by reinforcement the probability of a repetition of the same behaviour in similar circumstances is increased. Reinforcer and environment, together, can control the behaviour after a few repetitions. (Lefrancois, p. 34) Skinner distinguishes positive and negative reinforcement, with reinforcement being all stimuli that increase the

6

probability of the occurrence of a certain reaction, positive by being added to the situation, negative by taken out of it. The same considerations hold true for punishment, which decreases the probability for the re-occurrence of a reaction, either by adding a negative stimulus after the reaction or by taking a positive away. (Lefrancois, p. 34f)

To train rats and pigeons to behave in a certain way, Skinner invented a strategy called 'shaping'. An incidental behaviour that is somehow similar to the target behaviour or an aspect of a complex target behaviour is reinforced. The reinforcement is repeated and narrowed down to the actual target behaviour until the animal arrives at this trained behaviour subsequently. (Lefrancois, p. 41)

An important ability is to be able to generalise and discriminate different situations. Transferring a reaction to similar situations is necessary, because everybody is faced with numerous unknown situations every day and only reactions to very few of them can be learned in advance. Discrimination is the ability to distinguish between two similar but different situations, making people able to react in an appropriate way. (Lefrancois, p. 44)

According to Skinner, 'verbal behaviour' can be influenced by reinforcement as well. Greenspoon (1955) showed this in an experiment: a person was interviewed and asked to say some random words. He started talking, not knowing what to say, and each time he uttered a plural noun, he was reinforced by the interviewer saying 'hm'. In the course of the experiment, the probability for plural nouns to occur increased remarkably. (Lefrancois, p. 42) With the same strategy it is possible to influence the topics of a conversation by reinforcing one topic, i.e. by showing interest when the topic is mentioned and saying nothing otherwise. (Lefrancois, p. 42)

Skinner goes much further than these examples by stating that all language use and acquisition can be explained with his behaviouristic approach. For this, he extends his theory and terms of conditioning to human 'verbal behavior'. Skinner tries to identify the variables which control verbal behaviour and to find out how they interact, leading to a specific response (Chomsky 1959, p. 25). In analogy to his animal experimentation Skinner wants

to "provide a way to predict and control verbal behaviour by observing and manipulating the physical environment of the speaker". (Chomsky 1959, p.25)

It is not only verbal behaviour, "behaviour reinforced through the mediation of other persons" (Skinner, p. 2) in general, Skinner wants to explain with his approach, but also how this ability to communicate verbally is acquired.

Children hear a language being used in their environment and start to imitate certain sequences, repeating words and sentences they hear in their environment. This operant behaviour is reinforced by parents who pay attention to their children saying something, encouraging them to go on. Later they are reinforced by getting what they ask for, e.g. a toy (positive reinforcement) or food, stopping the child being hungry (negative reinforcement). By reinforcing or even punishing their child selectively, parents or other persons can shape his or her verbal behaviour concerning the knowledge of words, phrases and sentences. This history of reinforcement, together with a present stimulus, account for a person's verbal behaviour in every situation. (Skinner, p. 31, 203/4)

According to Skinner all kinds of human and animal learning can be explained and influenced by Behaviourism or, more precise, Operant Conditioning. For Skinner there seems to be no fundamental difference in the learning process between a rat, learning to press a lever to get a food pellet or to escape an electric shock and a child acquiring a language.


c    **Chomsky's Criticism**

In his article "A Review of B. F. Skinner's Verbal Behavior", Chomsky criticises Skinners work on human verbal ability. Chomsky does not argue against Skinner's behaviouristic studies in general, but makes clear why he thinks it is not appropriate to transfer conclusions and learning theories developed by studying the behaviour of rats and pigeons to explain human language use and acquisition. He is of the opinion that in Skinners laboratory experiments the notions of operant and response, among others, are perfectly reasonable and definable, but that transferring them to human behaviour and trying to use them out of highly controlled experimental situations with ordinary verbal behaviour is unreasonable, leaving the notions meaningless. (Chomsky 1959, p. 30) Chomsky repeatedly criticizes the loss of objectivity of Skinner's

theory, in general and especially of the basic concepts 'stimulus' (p. 29), 'response' (p. 30) and 'reinforcement' (p. 33), and by this the loss of all explanatory force. Although Chomsky values Skinner's advances concerning behaviouristic experiments on animal behaviour in his laboratory, he comes to the conclusion that Skinners theory is of no use explaining verbal behaviour or language acquisition. He tries to show that Skinners "description covers almost no aspect of verbal behaviour" if the terms are taken literally and is not superior to traditional formulations, taken metaphorically. (Chomsky 1959, p. 45) An example for this loss of objectivity would be that stimuli can only account for the wide range of possible verbal reactions by giving up the idea of their objectivity and considering that every person associates different things or ideas with a given stimulus. Only after hearing the response it is possible to identify the stimulus or property of the stimulus that induced it. (Chomsky 1959, p. 29) "Since any two objects have indefinitely many properties in common, we can be certain that we will never be at loss to explain a response of the form *A is like B*, for arbitrary A and B." (Chomsky 1959, p.42) It is impossible to predict the response to a certain stimulus and by this, it is impossible to predict or control verbal behaviour, except in very artificial cases.

Chomsky does not only criticize the way Skinner describes human language use and acquisition but also argues against basic assumptions and conclusions Skinner uses, dealing with human language in a behaviouristic context.

Chomsky's main point is Skinner's lack of interest in the organism itself with its internal structure, concentrating only on external factors. If internal factors were considered, the direct analogies to animal behaviour might become questionable. (Chomsky 1959, p. 26) In his view, children's special learning abilities are crucial to language acquisition and "...a refusal to study the contribution of the child to language learning permits only a superficial account of language acquisition..." (Chomsky 1959, p. 47) In Chomsky's view, simple conditioning is insufficient to account for all the diverse and complex aspects of human verbal ability (Chomsky 1959, p.43) and can only be applied to human behaviour in a very superficial way and not to behaviour involving higher mental faculties (Chomsky 1959, p.26/7)

Although Chomsky agrees, that children acquire a great amount of their verbal and nonverbal skills by observing adults and other children he does not share Skinner's statement that children learn language only through their parents "careful, differential reinforcement". (Chomsky 1959, p. 36) In his view, children learn language from various sources, without being taught explicitly. Chomsky emphasizes that reinforcement does play a significant role in language acquisition but he states that other factors, for example motivational ones, are of importance, too. He stresses

> the remarkable capacity of the child to generalize, hypothesize, and 'process information' in a variety of very special and apparently highly complex ways which we cannot yet describe or begin to understand, and which may be largely innate, or may develop through some sort of learning or through maturation of the nervous system. (Chomsky 1959, p.36)

Chomsky states that it is too early to develop a complex theory or 'functional analysis' of verbal behaviour without a better understanding what knowledge of a language really is and beyond this, how it is acquired. (Chomsky 1959, p. 45) First the structure of grammars must be known before one can try to account for the verbal behaviour of people speaking or learning a language. (Chomsky 1959, p.47) Concerning grammar use, he criticizes Skinners view that, in sentence formation, first the words are chosen and then arranged, as for him

> (i)t is evident that more is involved in sentence structure than insertion of lexical items in grammatical frames; no approach to language that fails to take these deeper processes into account can possibly achieve much success in accounting for actual linguistic behaviour. (Chomsky 1959, p. 44f)

He states that speakers have the ability to identify grammatical and ungrammatical sentences and understand unknown sentences. (Chomsky 1959, p. 36) Chomsky does not believe this happens simply by comparing new sentences with already known ones, "but because it is generated by the grammar that each individual has somehow and in some form internalized."(Chomsky 1959, p. 46)

He says that this grammar is highly complex and abstract and that all children acquire it in a very short period of time, in a similar way and largely independent of intelligence. These facts "suggest that human beings are somehow specially designed to do this". According to Chomsky, a theory of learning should take this into account. (Chomsky 1959, p.47)

# III.   Chomsky's Universal Grammar approach

Chomsky himself faces the challenge of developing a theory of language and language acquisition that takes all his criticism into account. Many basic ideas which led to his approach were therefore already mentioned in the previous chapter. In contrast to Skinner, he does not attempt to explain all language behaviour, but tries to find an explanation of what 'grammar' actually is and how humans come to know it. Chomsky finds it highly improbable that language learning could take place in a behaviouristic way and by this without any major contribution of the child. As said before, Chomsky does not believe knowledge of language to be a list of acceptable sentences or sentence structures but he is of the opinion that every native speaker of a language constructed a complex grammar, a representation of this language, in his or her mind during language acquisition.

Children are almost only confronted with acceptable sentences, they rarely hear wrong sentences and if they do, they do not get any information on why the sentence is not acceptable. This means they only have positive evidence and no negative. (Salkie, p. 37) Nevertheless, native speakers are able to judge whether a sentence they have never heard before is grammatical or not. This knowledge must be derived only from the positive evidence they were exposed to. (Salkie, p. 37) Children will be able to figure out rather obvious rules like, for example, the fact that adjectives precede nouns in English but it is not evident how they learn more complex rules like the Binding Principle, especially without having encountered any negative evidence. (Salkie, p. 36f, Crain, p. 19ff) This is called 'the logical problem of language acquisition' or 'poverty of the stimulus' and is the most important argument for language to be innate. In the limited input children acquiring a language get, there is not enough evidence to find out all the rules of their language's grammar. (Chomsky, 2002, p. 5ff) In an interview with Gliedman Chomsky gives an example of this. He states two sentences: "Which article did you file without reading (it)?" and "John was killed by a rock falling on him.".

Only in the first sentence pronoun dropping is possible, a 'parasitic gap' occurs. Such constructions are very rare and it is unlikely that a child ever heard them until he or she knows his or her language, but every adult knows whether a pronoun can be dropped without leaving an ungrammatical sentence. (Gliedman, p.2f)

Furthermore, Children learn their native language in an impressing short period of time and manage to construct a complete grammar of their language just on the basis of what they hear. This knowledge is very abstract and unconscious and in the end, after going through a series of almost identical acquisition steps, all children of a given speech community seem to arrive at a similar mental representation of their language. (Piattelli-Palmarini, p. 72)

From these points Chomsky concludes that humans must have some help acquiring language, some genetic endowment in the human mind, which assists children learning a language, accounting for the speed, systematicity and completeness of language acquisition. He came to the assumption that children are able to acquire the "rich and exotic grammatical knowledge" at such an early age because "knowledge is built in", because "we are designed to learn languages based upon a common set of principles, which we may call Universal Grammar". (Gliedman, p. 3) In contrast to Skinner, Chomsky does not only believe in general learning abilities a child is born with, but also in language-specific knowledge. Chomsky proposes that there are principles underlying all human languages and parameters, which can have two or more different values. These principles cover phonetic, syntactic, and semantic properties of language and, as a precondition for language acquisition, they are a part of the 'language faculty', which is one component of the mind. (Piattelli-Palmarini, p. 72f, 83)

An example of such a principle would be the head-principle with the possible parameter values 'head-left' or 'head-right'. All languages share the same principles, but whether or how a principle is realized differs among languages. It is this variation in possible composition of set parameters that makes a language unique. Every child is born with this Universal Grammar and acquiring a language means to 'fill' the principles, to turn the 'switches' on or off. (Chomsky, 1987, p. 68 quoted in Mitchell & Myles, p. 53) Children listen to their environment and build up some kind of grammar out of the input they get.

Learning a language, "(t)he language organ interacts with early experience and matures into the grammar of the language that the child speaks." (Gliedman, p. 1) As certain set parameters are supposed to "trigger" other parameter settings and all principles will induce their parameters to be set, this concept may well account for the astonishing speed of first language acquisition and it explains why, despite the rather random and sometimes defective input a child is exposed to, a full grammar is established by every single child. It also prevents the occurrence of any 'wild grammars' which cannot be found in native speaker grammars. It accounts for the fact that native speakers of a language can understand and construct an infinitive number of sentences which they have never heard before, meaning that they can use language in a highly creative way. Chomsky believes that language is innate to all humans, it is in our genes, like our outward appearance is and "the language organ grows like any other body organ" (Gliedman, p.1)

# IV. Piagets approach

Jean Piaget worked on a cognitive theory of development. His major concern was not language acquisition alone, but to find out about cognitive representations, focusing especially on how children's cognitive capacities gradually develop and come closer to the adult mental system. (Lefrancois, p. 122)

For Piaget the linguistic development cannot be seen as isolated, but language is "all of a piece with acquisitions made at the level of sensorimotor intelligence" (Piattelli-Palmarini, p. 163). Language is an indetachable part of a more general cognitive organisation and so is its development. (Gliedman, p. 5) The acquisition of language requires motor, perceptual and cognitive abilities. Especially cognitive capacities, to form concepts of permanent object, space, time, causality and the like, are crucial to language acquisition.

The acquisition of grammar is based on sensorimotor intelligence and the mental grammar itself is derived from general cognitive structures and rules. Piaget claims that "language appears at about the same time as the other forms of semiotic thought" (Piaget, 1969, p. 59) and that "there is a surprising degree of correlation between the language employed and the mode of reasoning" (Piaget, 1969, p. 61) In contrast to Chomsky, Piaget denies a rigid pre-programming as well as an independent status of language, though he does not deny the existence of innate entities in general. ( Piaget, 1969, p. 59, Inhelder, p.133) Piaget claims that "function can be innate, not structure". According to his approach, all human cognitive capacities develop simultaneously and this development is based on a kind of pre-set program, which is stimulated by the environment. To learn and develop the child has to interact with his or her environment. This interaction can be acoustical, visual or multiple. (Inhelder, p. 134) There are two versions of Jean Piaget's theory. Piaget's original 'strong version' claims that the cognitive prerequisites are a necessary but also sufficient condition for language acquisition to take place. So, all aspects of language are determined by the constructions of sensorimotor intelligence and there is a very strong interdependence between linguistic and general cognitive abilities. A weaker version, which was put forward  by Bärbel Inhelder and the

Geneva Group states that sensorimotor intelligence and cognitive representations are a necessary condition for language to emerge, but although linguistic and cognitive development interact in the beginning, linguistic development takes place in an independent and unique way, later. (Piattelli-Palmarini, p. 94f)

In its 'epistemological genesis' the child passes through four discrete stages. Within each of the stages important abilities are acquired, which prepare the child for the following stage. (Lefrancois, p.129, 131; Piattelli-Palmarini, p. 65f)

The first stage is the 'sensorimotor period', lasting from age 0 to age 2. The child starts to adapt to the environment in a physical way, also due to the fact that he or she has not yet the means to communicate verbally. The world is experienced in an egocentric way. Mental representations and the concept of permanent objects, which enables children to refer to objects that are not present only develop gradually as does the understanding of a 'logic of action'. Piaget mentions five 'behaviour patterns', which show that these concepts emerged and which are all based on imitation, namely 'deferred imitation', 'symbolic play', 'drawing', the 'mental image' as internalized imitation and the 'verbal evocation'. (Piaget, 1969, p. 57f) Language has a positive influence on the child's way of thinking and enables him or her to develop an increasingly cognitive interpretation of the environment. (Piaget, 1969, p. 60) At this stage children also develop a concept of causality and organization of space, in addition to the ability to symbolize and communicate. (Lefrancois, p. 130f, Piattelli-Palmarini, p. 65)

The second stage lasts from age 2 to 7 and is subdivided into Preoperational and Preconceptual Stage. After he or she developed mental representations of objects, the child starts to build classes and subclasses, although he or she is not able, yet, to understand all of the properties a given class has. This is why over- and undergeneralizations, as well as transductive thinking occur in the earlier phases of this stage. At the age of 4 to 7 children start to think in a more logical way, still being influenced by perception to a large part, as Piaget showed in his studies with children judging the content of water containers.

Although children are able to assign objects to classes, they are, however, not yet able to logically distinguish between classes and subclasses. (Lefrancois, p. 131ff)

During the third, 'Concrete Operational Stage', which lasts from age 7 to age 11/12 children start to think logically. They are capable of dealing with classes, series and numbers, although this capacity is restricted to concrete objects. In this context, children develop the concept of reversible operations and of conservation. (Lefrancois, p. 137; Piattelli-Palmarini, p. 65)

In the final, 'Formal Operational Stage', age 11/12 to 14/15, children develop hypothetic, logical and abstract thinking and learn to see different perspectives of an issue. (Lefrancois, p. 138) Obviously, the first two of these stages are of greater importance to linguists, as they cover the period in which most of the human language is acquired.

As mentioned above, children learn by interacting with the world, imitating and identifying with the people and objects surrounding them. Piaget calls this interactive learning process 'adaption'. It can be subdivided into 'assimilation' and 'accomodation'. Assimilating, the child reacts on the surrounding world by applying already acquired reactions to an unknown, but similar object or situation. If it is not possible to assimilate the new situation the child has to change his or her behaviour, developing a new scheme. This process is called accommodation. (Lefrancois, p. 124ff, 129) These schemes and concepts are constantly altered and developed further, as every action includes assimilation and accommodation. By this, learning is a progressive and active construction on the basis of existing knowledge. The process does not stop at the end of childhood, but assimilation and accommodation are used during the entire life. (Lefrancois, p. 125f)

Piaget believes that language is structured by logic. (Piaget 1969, p. 62) This logic can already be seen at the sensorimotor stage, before language occurs, as a 'logic in action'. Existing schemes of action are linked and subschemes emerge. Piaget judges these phenomena as indicating the development of human logic and argues that the schemes of assimilation are 'practical concepts' preceding mental representation. (Piattelli-Palmarini, p. 91)

After children manage to assimilate objects with certain properties into 'schemes of action', assimilation between the objects themselves emerges. This new assimilation allows conceptual logic but requires evocation, the child needs to develop mental representation of objects which are not present. This is made possible by the development of the symbolic function, of which language is one particular case. Imitation, copying characteristics of objects by using gestures, plays an important role in the development of the semiotic function, as "... it continues later on as an interiorized imitation that creates the ensuing representations." (Piattelli-Palmarini, p. 91f) This imitation, which can already be observed from the age of 8 months on (Rieber, p. 114), seems to be of great importance in this learning theory, not only to acquire concepts of deferred objects. Piaget states also that language is "necessarily acquired in a context of imitation", for if it would be acquired by conditioning, as Skinner proposed, language would occur at a much earlier age. (Piaget 1969, p. 58)

The child proceeds from one stage to another with the use of abstraction, reorganizing the existing knowledge. (Piattelli-Palmarini, p.67) The transition from the first to the second stage is due to the development of the semiotic function. During the sensorimotor stage objects are assimilated into known schemes, while in the preoperational period conceptual schemes are constructed by assimilating objects to each other using representative assimilation. This is only possible if the concept of object permanence, a part of the semiotic function, has already been acquired. (Piattelli-Palmarini, p. 68)

The influence between general cognition and language is not only directed in one way, but language is also important for the further development of thought, because it enables interpersonal exchange and cooperation and therewith social regulation. By this, language and thought are not only interrelated but even "linked in a genetic circle". (Inhelder, p. 134)

# V. The debate between Chomsky and Piaget

As Chomsky's criticism made quite clear, a behaviouristic learning theory is not sufficient to account for a child's first language acquisition, a point Chomsky and Piaget both agree on. (Piattelli-Palmarini, p. 86) Although Skinners theory was once widely accepted and valued, the ideas behind it did not hold until today. In contrast to the behaviouristic theory, the arguments and ideas which constitute Chomsky's and Piaget's language acquisition theories are, thought altered and developed further, still present in many current approaches. After the three fundamental theories of language acquisition have been presented, the basic assumptions Chomsky and Piaget built their theories on will be contrasted and some counterarguments Piaget and Chomsky provide against each others assumptions will be highlighted.

Chomsky believes in the mind being divided into certain modules, which develop independently. Piaget does not share this view, but argues for a general cognitive organization with all mental capacities developing interdependently.

As it was said above, Chomsky believes in a 'modular mind'. The mind consists of several faculties, one of them being the 'language faculty' or 'language organ', as he puts it. In his opinion 'mental organs' and body organs develop in similar ways and it is only "a curiosity of our intellectual history that cognitive structures developed by the mind are generally regarded and studied very differently from physical structures developed by the body." (Piattelli-Palmarini, p. 74) Chomsky sees many analogies between mental and body organs. The body organs grow at their own rates, interacting, but not depending on each other in their development and so, he believes, do the mental organs. (Gliedman, p. 6)

Piaget argues that the human development takes place in four distinct stages. Each stage is defined by the occurrence of a certain kind of constructive development. All cognitive capacities develop in an analogous way and when the characteristic abilities of one phase are acquired, the child moves on to the

next stage. Assimilation, which is visible from birth is the general learning mechanism, "(t)he fundamental relationship that constitutes all knowledge ...". (Piattelli-Palmarini, p. 64f) Studies showed that deaf children go through the stages of logical development with a delay of one or two years. This might support Piaget's view, as language is supposed to have an impact on the mental development. Studies with blind children showed that, though the verbal development was quite normal, they had serious problems dealing with the relationship of order and topological positions. Piaget reads this as a proof for his thesis that 'action learning' is of crucial importance and can not be compensated by 'verbal coordinations'. (Rieber, p. 116f)

Piaget argues that language, as a part of the semiotic function, appears in the second stage of his development schedule and, thus, profits from all the acquisitions in terms of sensorimotor intelligence and symbolic function that have already been made. (Piattelli-Palmarini, p. 92) From the synchronous occurrence of language and the other parts of the semiotic function, Piaget derives one of the strongest arguments for his theory of a general cognitive development and against Chomsky's theory of a modular mind, namely that he can account for the age at which language emerges. He argues that if language was learned through conditioning, it would occur much earlier and that a theory of innateness has no means to explain why language acquisition takes place at a certain age. (Rieber, p. 113; Piattelli-Palmarini, p. 93) Chomsky debilitates this argument, saying that there are several events in human life, like puberty or death, which seem to happen scheduled, just like language acquisition does. (Gliedman, p. 2)

Chomsky believes in an innate language acquisition device containing Universal Grammar, which enables all humans to learn a native language, the language of the speech community they grow up in. Piaget does not agree with Chomsky, as he does not see the necessity or any biological explanation for the innateness of language.

Piaget has two main arguments against Chomsky's thesis of an innate grammar. The first of these arguments is that the mutations which must have led to these innate structures are "biologically inexplicable" He argues that if

language and reason were innate, they would have developed as a chain of random mutations, a process which would still be going on. He finds it already quite astonishing that the human language system emerged out of these mutations and cannot believe that some Universal Grammar might emerge out of a random process. (Piattelli-Palmarini, p.69f) As for Piaget language and other cognitive capacities are strongly interrelated, the idea of innateness affects the concept of the origin of other mental abilities. Because the child, as a human being, is only the outcome of a long process of development, Piaget argues, one would have to look for the origins of such an endowment in protozoa and viruses. For him "the theories of preformation of knowledge appear...as devoid of concrete truth as empiricist interpretations, for the origin of logico-mathematical structures in their infinity cannot be localized either in objects or in the subject." (Piattelli-Palmarini, p. 66) He rejects the idea that reason and therefore also logico-mathematical structures might have developed by chance, but points out that their origin can only lie in "an exact and detailed adaption to reality". He proposes an explanation of the development with the notion of phenocopies. A being changes in an improving way, and others of the same kind reconstruct this change genetically. By this innateness does not necessarily need to be a random process. (Piattelli-Palmarini, p. 87) This system could even work without any genetical change at all, as the phenotypic change and the copying of this behaviour could take place in every generation anew. (Piattelli-Palmarini, p. 88)

Piaget's second argument against an innate language endowment is that language acquisition can as well be explained as "the 'necessary' result of constructions of sensorimotor intelligence" (Piattelli-Palmarini, p. 73) and therefore there is no need for innateness. He argues that during the sensorimotor period, at the end of which language occurs, the child "constructs" enough knowledge to account for the emergence and development of language acquisition (Piattelli-Palmarini, p. 87), so that the 'fixed nucleus' of language we all share is simply based on the children's biological development, sufficient to account for language acquisition. (Rieber, p. 109, Piattelli-Palmarini, p. 87)

Chomsky replies to Piaget's arguments, stating that although the evolutionary development remains 'unexplained' it does not need to be 'inexplicable'. Chomsky continues his argument comparing language with the

physical organs of the human body, whose development we can only try to explain in retrospective, without knowing exactly how it took place and why they developed in exactly this way and not in alternative possible manners. It might be unclear how the 'language organ' developed by random mutations, but the same holds true for other organs, as well. He argues that this fact did not lead scientists to argue that organs, like the human eye, developed through interaction with the environment. (Piattelli-Palmarini, p. 73)

With regard to Piaget's second argument Chomsky states that there is no relation between the linguistic principles he found and the constructions of sensorimotor intelligence, therefore he rejects Piaget's strong position. He points out that he can agree with Inhelder's weaker position, in that some of the properties of language use and structure originate in sensorimotor construction, as he believes that some aspects of language acquisition relate to general cognitive development, but he stresses, that he is particularly interested in those properties which are unique to language. (Piattelli-Palmarini, p. 90) Although he does not deny Inhelder's weaker hypothesis straight away he argues that, as blind children acquire language not slowlier but even quicker than healthy children and he can not imagine paralegic or paralysed children having specific problems acquiring language, there is no reason to maintain this weaker thesis. In this context Chomsky mentions an even weaker thesis put forward by Fodor, namely that the development of action schemes might have a triggering function for the acquisition of language. Chomsky states that the only arguments for this thesis are the orderly progression of sensorimotor functions and language and some not very general similarities, which do not relate to the language principles. This is why he concludes that language is structured and organized in a unique way, without any analogies to other cognitive domains and this organization is part of the initial state. (Piattelli-Palmarini, p. 73, 94ff, Chomsky, 1986, p. 22) Another of Chomsky's arguments against the interdependent development of the constructivist approach to language acquisition and for an innate 'language acquisition device' is the complexity of language and the mental grammar. The intellectual capacities needed to grasp the complex system of a language go far beyond those shown by a child in other areas. "And these abilities are independent of the logical capacities measured by tests."(Gliedman, p. 6)

For Jean Piaget, the uniform development of children, passing through discrete and predictable stages can be interpreted in two ways. They could either mean "authentic constructions with stepwise disclosures to new possibilities or successive actualisation of a set of possibilities *existing from the beginning.*" (Piattelli-Palmarini, p. 66) Either the child 'reconstructs operations' and 'reinvents' the basics of logic and mathematics or performs what he or she was genetically endowed with. With the arguments stated above he rules out the latter possibility for his theory. As a conclusion, only a constructivist learning approach can account for the children's development, as far as Piaget is concerned. (Piattelli-Palmarini, p. 66) He believes, that children's cognitive development, including language, is a process of systematic constructivism. Nevertheless there must be some basic knowledge to start out with. (Piattelli-Palmarini, p. 68) Piaget says that all behaviours are based on an innate and an acquired component, although it might be difficult to say where exactly the boundary is. According to Piaget 'something' concerning functioning is innate, but in contrast to Chomsky he does not believe in any innate structures. (Piattelli-Palmarini, p. 93) Piaget believes in certain inborn conditions that help to build intelligence (Rieber, p. 111) by which „...the functioning of intelligence alone is hereditary and creates structures only through an organization of successive actions performed on objects". (Piattelli-Palmarini, p. 64f) Whereas the functioning of cognition is inborn, cognitive structures have to be constructed successively by autoregulation. (Piattelli-Palmarini, p. 88) Piaget argues that such autoregulatory processes, opposed to a genetic language acquisition device developed by chance, are common in biological and mental functions. (Piattelli-Palmarini, p. 69)

# VI.  Conclusion

Although Chomsky and Piaget can not reach an agreement on the crucial questions of whether or not extensive innate help acquiring the native language is needed and whether the acquisition is interdependent with other cognitive development they do agree on the point that language cannot be the product of behaviouristic conditioning but of reason and that there must be a fixed cognitive structure, which is needed to learn any language, either innate or constructed. Piaget "can go so far as to say that on the issue relating to the relationships between language and thought, [he] consider[s himself] to be in symmetry with Chomsky", a statement Chomsky agrees on as well. (Piattelli-Palmarini, p. 86, 89) To reach a minimal consensus, Piaget states he would be satisfied with a compromise proposed by Changeux at the Royaumont Symposium 1975, saying that in addition to a genetic endowment activity plays an important role in the child's mental development. (Rieber, p. 110)

The aim of this paper was not primarily to judge the positions that were presented, or to find the language acquisition theory which is most likely to be true, but to show how the three basic theories concerning language acquisition emerged and what their founder's original arguments were. Both positions, nativism and cognitivism, were developed further by many linguists, studying in the field of language acquisition. Linguists still argue how language acquisition and general cognitive development are related and have not come to a consensus concerning kind and structure of an inborn language learning endowment, although the majority of linguists believes in some kind of genetic predisposition. However, there are not two opposed groups of current theories but a variety of different views, some of them based on ideas taken from both, Chomsky's and Piaget's original approach.

# VII. Bibliography:

**Chomsky, Noam**. 1959. "A Review of Skinner's Verbal Behavior."
2004. Lust, Barbara et al. *First Language Acquisition: The Essential Readings*. Oxford: Blackwell Publishing. pp. 25-55

**Chomsky, Noam**. 1986. "Knowledge of Language as a Focus of Inquiry."
2004. Lust, Barbara et al. *First Language Acquisition: The Essential Readings*. Oxford: Blackwell Publishing. pp. 15-24

**Chomsky, Noam**. 2002. *On Nature and Language*. Cambridge: Cambridge University Press

**Crain, Stephen and Rosalind Thornton**. 1998. *Investigations in Universal Grammar: A guide to experiments on the Acquisition of syntax*. Massachusetts: MIT Press

**Inhelder, Bärbel**, "Language and Knowledge in a Constructivist Framework." 1980. Piattelli-Palmarini , Massimo (ed.). *Language and Learning, The Debate between Jean Piaget and Noam Chomsky*. Cambridge. Massachusetts: Harvard University Press

**Lefrancois, Guy**. 1994. *Psychologie des Lernens*. 3. Auflage. Berlin: Springer-Verlag

**Mitchell, Rosamond & Florence Myles**. 1998. *Second Language Learning Theories*. London: Arnold, Hodder Headline Group

**Piaget, Jean and Bärbel Inhelder**. 1969. "The Semiotic or Symbolic Function" Lust, Barbara et al. *First Language Acquisition: The Essential Readings*. Oxford: Blackwell Publishing. pp. 56-63

**Piattelli-Palmarini, Massimo**. (ed.). 1980. "Language and Learning, The Debate between Jean Piaget and Noam Chomsky Lust, Barbara et al. *First Language Acquisition: The Essential Readings*. Oxford: Blackwell Publishing. pp. 64-97

**Rieber, R. W.** (ed.). 1983. *Dialogues on the Psychology of Language and Thought*. New York and London: Plenum Press

**Salkie , Raphael**. 1990. *The Chomsky update Linguistics and Politics*. London: Unwin Hyman

**Skinner, B.F.** 1957. *Verbal Behavior.* New York: Appleton Century Crofts

Interview:

**Gliedman, J.** 11/1983. „Things no amount of learning can teach ." Noam Chomsky interviewed by John Gliedman; Omni, 6:11.
www. Chomsky. info/interviews (02.12.2006)

9 783638 911566